IMPRESSIONS *of the*

PEAK DISTRICT

Produced by AA Publishing
© Automobile Association Developments Limited 2007

Published by AA Publishing (a trading name of Automobile Association
Developments Limited, whose registered office is Fanum House, Basing View,
Basingstoke, Hampshire RG21 4EA; registered number 1878835)

ISBN-10: 0-7495-5210-7
ISBN-13: 978-0-7495-5210-7

A03033B

A CIP catalogue record for this book is available from the British Library.

The contents of this book are believed correct at the time of printing. Nevertheless,
the publishers cannot be held responsible for any errors, omissions or for changes in
the details given in this book or for the consequences of any reliance on the
information provided by the same. This does not affect your statutory rights.

Colour reproduction by KDP, Kingsclere
Printed and bound in Thailand by Sirivatana Interprint Public Co Ltd

Opposite: striding across giant boulders at the top of Kinder Downfall.

IMPRESSIONS *of the*
PEAK DISTRICT

Picture Acknowledgements

The Automobile Association wishes to thank the following photographers, companies
and picture libraries for their assistance in the preparation of this book.

Abbreviations for the picture credits are as follows: (AA) AA World Travel Library

3 AA/T Mackie; 5 AA/T Mackie; 7 AA/T Mackie; 8 AA/T Mackie; 9 AA/T Mackie; 10 AA/N Coates; 11 AA/T
Mackie; 12 AA/T Mackie; 13 AA/T Mackie; 14 AA/T Mackie; 15 AA/T Mackie; 16 AA/T Mackie; 17 AA/T Mackie;
18 AA/T Mackie; 19 AA/A J Hopkins; 20 AA; 21 AA/T Mackie; 22 AA/T Mackie; 23 AA/M Birkitt; 24 AA/T
Mackie; 25 AA/A J Hopkins; 26 AA/T Mackie; 27 AA/T Mackie; 28 AA/T Mackie; 29 AA/T Mackie; 30 AA/J
Beazley; 31 AA/P Baker; 32 AA/T Mackie; 33 AA/P Baker; 34 AA/T Mackie; 35 AA/T Mackie; 36 AA/T Mackie; 37
AA/T Mackie; 38 AA/A Midgely; 39 AA/T Mackie; 40 AA/T Mackie; 41 AA/A Tryner; 42 AA/J Welsh; 43 AA/J
Beazley; 44 AA/T Mackie; 45 AA/T Mackie; 46 AA/T Mackie; 47 AA/T Mackie; 48 AA/N Coates; 49 AA/P Baker; 50
AA/N Coates; 51 AA/T Mackie; 52 AA/T Mackie; 53 AA/M Birkitt; 54 AA/T Mackie; 55 AA/T Mackie; 56 AA/T
Mackie; 57 AA/T Mackie; 58 AA/T Mackie; 59 AA/A Midgely; 60 AA/T Mackie; 61 AA/T Mackie; 62 AA/T Mackie;
63 AA/T Mackie; 64 AA/T Mackie; 65 AA/T Mackie; 66 AA/T Mackie; 67 AA/T Mackie; 68 AA/T Mackie; 69 AAA
Midgely; 70 AA/A J Hopkins; 71 AA/T Mackie; 72 AA/T Mackie; 73 AA/T Mackie; 74 AA/T Mackie; 75 AA/T
Mackie; 76 AA/N Coates; 77 AA/T Mackie; 78 AA/P Bennett; 79 AA/T Mackie; 80 AA/T Mackie; 81 AA/T Mackie;
82 AA/T Mackie; 83 AA/N Coates; 84 AA/T Mackie; 85 AA/T Mackie; 86 AA/T Mackie; 87 AA/T Mackie

Every effort has been made to trace the copyright holders, and we apologise in advance for any unintentional
omissions or errors. We would be happy to apply the corrections in any following edition of this publication.

*Opposite: the spire of All Saints Parish Church towers above Bakewell. Although some parts date back to
Norman times, much of the church was rebuilt in the 1840s.*

INTRODUCTION

Sandwiched between the urban sprawls of southwest Yorkshire, Manchester and the east and north Midlands, 20 million people live within an hour's drive of the Peak District. Stretching from the green lowlands of the Midlands to the high moors of the South Pennines, this is a vital slice of countryside for so many people it is a wonder that it has survived the onslaught. But survived it has, and much of the credit for that goes to the Peak District National Park – it was the first area in Britain to receive this designation, in 1951.

The park covers 555sq miles (1,438sq km), and although mostly in Derbyshire, it also strays well into Cheshire, Greater Manchester, Staffordshire and Yorkshire. From the bleak, high moors of the northerly Dark Peak, famed for the Pennine Way, Kinder Scout and the Upper Derwent reservoirs, the park spills south into the verdant limestone uplands of the White Peak, where Dovedale, Monsal Dale, Lathkill Dale and the Manifold Valley are the undoubted stars. There are picturebook villages such as Hartington and Tissington, and those with a more complex claim to history, such as the 'plague village' of Eyam.

The stresses on the area's countryside aren't just from tourism. Mining, quarrying, water catchment and forestry have all put pressure on a landscape that we have slowly learned to treasure. Now much of the Peak District's industrial heritage has become an attraction in itself. The great reservoirs of the Upper Derwent Valley are so popular with visitors that traffic management schemes have had to be introduced to retain some semblance of peace and tranquillity at weekends.

But despite the proximity of so many people, it is still possible to find solitude here, and that is perhaps why so many return again and again. You might be striding out along the fine moorland ridges above Edale, or exploring the hidden limestone dales in the White Peak; you might take a boat out onto Carsington Water or wander the gardens of Chatsworth House or Haddon Hall – the Peaks appeal to almost everyone. And much of the fringe of this protected sphere is no less pretty. The market and spa town of Buxton boasts fine architecture; Matlock, Matlock Bath and Wirksworth are fascinating to explore, and at Cromford, Richard Arkwright's pioneering 18th-century mills are so historically important that UNESCO has designated them a World Heritage Site.

The character of the region's landscape has always made it attractive to film-makers and its historic homes and ageless scenery often crop up on television. In the far north east, where the Dark Peak merges into the South Pennines, the gentle sitcom *The Last of the Summer Wine* evoked images of a second childhood for a generation. Recent TV and film adaptations of Charlotte Brontë's *Jane Eyre* and Jane Austen's *Pride and Prejudice* have both drawn heavily on Peakland landscapes.

For many visitors the Peak District conjures up images of bobble-hatted walkers, peculiar caves and flower bedecked wells. But this most-visited of English National Parks has a great deal more to offer.

Ladybower was the last of the three reservoirs that flooded the Upper Derwent Valley. It was completed in 1943 and took two more years to fill.

The cliffs and pinnacles at Kinder Downfall mark the edge of the vast moorland plateau of Kinder Scout.
Opposite: walkers in Cressbrook Dale near Litton, one of five valleys that make up the Derbyshire Dales National Nature Reserve.

Looking down an old farm track near the Manifold Valley.
Opposite: blackfaced sheep above Kinder Downfall. Grazing in this sensitive upland habitat is tightly managed to prevent further erosion of the fragile peat bogs.

Ivy and roses clad a cottage wall in Ashford in the Water. The annual well dressing celebrates the village's close relationship with its six natural springs.

This 18th-century sundial is mounted over a doorway in St Lawrence's Church, Eyam. The village is best remembered for the heroic isolation of its inhabitants during the great plague of 1665. Led by the Rector William Mompesson, nearly half the village lived for over a year in self-imposed quarantine, in an attempt to halt the spread of the disease. Over 200 died, including the rector's wife Katherine, before the outbreak subsided.

The tea room next door to 'Nora Battie's house' in Holmfirth celebrates this icon from The Last of the Summer Wine.
*Opposite: the River Wye flows quickly over a weir in Monsal Dale. Early industry relied on water power,
and the valley is littered with these reminders of its working past.*

Traffic is restricted on a quiet road beside the Upper Derwent reservoirs.
Opposite: the Roaches are a highlight of Staffordshire's part of the Peak District. They take their name from the French 'roches', meaning rocks,
and are extremely popular with climbers.

Brindley Mill and pond in Leek. Built by canal pioneer James Brindley in 1752, the mill was restored in the 1970s.

Opposite: the limestone uplands above the Manifold Valley are criss-crossed by drystone walls, many from the 18th- and early 19th-century enclosures.

Evening sunlight on sailing dinghies in Errwood Reservoir. The second of the Goyt Valley lakes, it was built to supply water to Stockport in the 1960s.

Crossing a wooden bridge over the fast-flowing River Wye in Miller's Dale.

You can call in to the real Sid's Cafe in Holmfirth, and re-enact your favourite scenes from The Last of the Summer Wine.

Narrow strip fields like these near Chelmorton, divided by stone walls, may betray their origins in the medieval period as strips in an open field.

The Peak District was a formidable barrier to early road builders. Here a milestone shows the distance
to Sheffield and Manchester on an 18th-century turnpike route.
Opposite: a pink evening light softens Curbar Edge above the Derwent Valley.

A curving staircase takes you to the upper deck of a restored tram at Crich Tramway Village,
home of the National Tramway Museum.

Ollerbrook Booth, Edale, surrounded by green fields below the looming mass of Edale Moor.

This green tram at Crich Tramway Village was built for Liverpool Corporation in 1936. It stands next to a more ornate Chesterfield Corporation tram from 1904.
Opposite: meadowland in the White Peak. These rich limestone uplands, here above the Manifold Valley, support a wide range of wild flowers.

The celebrated Bakewell pudding may have been invented by accident in the town of Bakewell in the 19th century. The first shop to sell them has now become a shrine for pudding fans from all parts of the world.

Opposite: Pilsbury is a remote hamlet in the upper reaches of the Dove Valley.

The magnificent gardens at Haddon Hall near Bakewell were restored in the 1920s by the 9th Duke and Duchess of Rutland. Opposite: storm clouds gather over the Peakland landscape seen from Curbar Edge.

Drystone walls divide the fields in both the White and the Dark Peak. The capstones here deflect the elements from the heart of the wall, preventing frost damage.

Thor's Cave in the Manifold Valley. This prominent limestone cavern was occupied in Palaeolithic times, and may contain up to seven different burial sites.

Cottage gardens near Matlock, framed by trees. The local gritstone produces a warm coloured building stone that characterises buildings in this corner of the Peak District.

Sympathetic planting on the shores of Howden Reservoir in the Upper Derwent Valley has produced a sylvan landscape. The lake is contained by the Howden Dam and was completed in 1912 to supply water to the East Midlands.

A photographer's shop from the early 1900s is just one of those re-created in the Crich Tramway Village. Other buildings include the Red Lion pub, moved brick by brick from its former site opposite a tram depot in Stoke-on-Trent. Opposite: paving prevents erosion on the sensitive summit of Mam Tor.

A cottage garden at Tissington in the White Peak. Much of the village was created by the FitzHerbert family around their country house estate – Tissington Hall.

Looking down Dovedale from the strangely conical limestone peak of Thorpe Cloud.

High up among the Staffordshire moorlands, Flash was once a notorious base for forgers, producing 'flash money'.

Strolling by the River Dove at sunset. You may recognise the scene from several TV period dramas.

Wirksworth was once a prosperous lead-mining centre and is now a busy market town.
Opposite: from the summit trig point on Mam Tor the view stretches beyond the limestone gorge of
Winnats, over the high green fields of the White Peak to the fringe of gritstone crags beyond.

Cromford Mill (1771), the first in the world to harness water to power factory-scale spinning machines, is at the heart of the Derwent Valley Mills World Heritage Site.

Reflections on Ladybower Reservoir, a two-fingered lake in the Woodlands and Upper Derwent valleys.

Carsington Water's sculpture trail depicts the valley's history prior to the reservoir's completion in 1992.

The River Wye at Bakewell, the only town within the National Park boundary, and sometimes known as the 'Capital of the Peak'.

Close Gate Bridge, a packhorse bridge on an old route across the moors to Rochdale.

Opposite: looking across Edale into the valley of Grindsbrook and the starting point of the Pennine Way National Trail.

Climbing on the Roaches. The British Mountaineering Council owns a climbing hut beneath these gritstone crags, named after the pioneering climber Don Whillans.

Bakewell puddings probably pre-date the claims of the Original Bakewell Pudding Shop,
but the different recipes are still jealously guarded secrets.

Fishing boats moored on Ladybower Reservoir. Fly fishing for wild trout is a popular Peakland pastime.

A lion's head spews out warm water from St Ann's Well, a thermal spring in Buxton.

Looking up the Holme Valley, Holmfirth – Last of the Summer Wine *country.*
Opposite: big skies above the peat and bog morass that forms most of the 2,000ft (600m) Kinder Scout Plateau.

The summit of Mam Tor was once occupied by a hillfort, with its origins in the Bronze Age. A popular destination for tourists, the hill's proximity to a main road, and its outstanding views, have contributed to the erosion of this fragile landscape.

Stepping stones across the river, beneath Thorpe Cloud, Dovedale.

Colourful hanging baskets on a row of cottages in Grindleford. The village became a popular destination for urban Sheffield folk when the railway arrived through the Totley tunnel in 1893.

Curbar Edge's gritstone blocks offer great views for walkers and some famously testing challenges for rock climbers.

Thick ivy covers a cottage wall in the estate village of Tissington.

Opposite: watersports enthusiasts enjoy a blustery day on Carsington Water. The reservoir is supplied by water extracted from the River Derwent at Ambergate in the winter months. A 6½-mile (10.5km) aqueduct connects the river to the lake.

Looking across the Manifold Valley to Grindon, Staffordshire, and the spire of All Saints' Church. The opening to Thor's Cave can be seen in the foreground.

The Howden Dam, framed by trees and flowering rhododendrons in early summer. Completed in 1912, the dramatic spillway allows water from the reservoir to pour over the top of the dam in very wet weather.

The Church of St John the Baptist in Tideswell is one of the largest in the area and is often referred to as the 'Cathedral of the Peak'.
Replacing an earlier Norman church, it was completed in 1400 and has had few alterations since.

Walkers enjoy the view from the summit of Mam Tor.

Looking along North Parade, Matlock Bath. The village grew as a resort in the 19th-century boom for hydropathic cures.

Reaching 298ft (91m), the Emperor Fountain in front of Chatsworth House is the tallest gravity-fed fountain in the world.

Could Little John have been buried beneath this yew tree in the graveyard at Hathersage? The grave is often well-tended.
Opposite: a narrow road descends through Winnats Pass into the Hope Valley near Castleton. The limestone pinnacles that
characterise the gorge were once the sides of an undersea ravine between two coral reefs.

On the way to the summit of the famous Snake Pass. The road reaches 1,680ft (512m), and despite its winding route, takes its name from the nearby Snake Inn.

Hanging baskets and roses make for a colourful shopping scene in Bakewell.

Looking across the Greyhound Pond to Cromford village. The pond supplied water to Arkwright's mills lower down the valley.

Bamford and Shatton in the Hope Valley. The hill behind is Shatton Edge, where the White and Dark Peak meet.

Cyclists on the High Peak Trail, passing old quarry workings near Minninglow.
Opposite: Riley Graves on the edge of Eyam. The simple headstones record the deaths of seven members of the Hancock family who succumbed to the bubonic plague one terrible week in August 1666.

Flowers in the garden at Haddon Hall. The house has been in the Manners family since 1567.

Along the ridge to Hollins Cross from Mam Tor.
This classic ridge walk extends to Lose Hill and is a favourite of many Peakland walkers.

The River Derwent winds its way through Matlock Bath. The steep sides of the gorge, with their giant crags, were a fascination to early tourists.

Black and red flowers picked out in the ironwork of the bandstand in the Pavilion Gardens, Buxton.
This 23-acre (9.3ha) municipal park was laid out in 1871 by Edward Milner, who also worked on the Crystal Palace, London.

Sailing dinghies on Torside Reservoir, Longdendale. This High Peak valley is dominated by five reservoirs and a major trans-Pennine route. Opposite: looking north into Upperdale from Monsal Head, the River Wye has snaked its way through several limestone gorges.

Fly fishing at sunset on Ladybower Reservoir in the Upper Derwent Valley.

Looking down on Matlock Bath, once described as a 'seaside resort without the sea'.

Buxton Opera House, built in 1903 and designed by Frank Matcham. Matcham was a prolific theatrical architect, putting his name to over 200 buildings all over the United Kingdom, including the London Palladium and the Grand Theatre, Blackpool.

Bluebells and wood anemones thrive in old coppice woods, Miller's Dale.

Sheepwash Well, one of the six wells in Ashford in the Water that will be decorated in the annual well-dressing festival around Trinity Sunday (late May/early June).

Art imitates life – an artificial waterfall drains a pond in the Pavilion Gardens, Buxton.

Detail of a 1904 Chesterfield Corporation tram, preserved and restored at Crich Tramway Village.
Opposite: Kinder Reservoir gleams in the distance, seen from the top of Kinder Downfall.

The lowered waterline betrays Howden Reservoir's true purpose, in an otherwise apparently natural scene from the Upper Derwent Valley.

The village green and pond in Tissington, popular with walkers, cyclists and ducks.

Boats on the Peak Forest Canal at Whaley Bridge. The canal linked into the Cheshire canal system, carrying limestone, coal, cotton and grain out of northwest Derbyshire.
Opposite: the sun sets in orange over the hills of the Hope Valley.

INDEX